First

GET HIS ATTENTION

and other stories from different traditions

Compiled and Edited by

L a r r y   C o h e n

PAGE PUBLISHING, INC.
Conneaut Lake, PA

First originally published by Page Publishing 2020

cover design by Larry Cohen. Cover illustration by Bruce Zeines
Photograph of Jerry Brewster by John Anderson. Illustrations
by Larry Cohen, Andy DeSantis, Ron Dixon, Dave Fishman,
and Bruce Zeines.

ISBN 978-1-6624-1128-1 (pbk)
ISBN 978-1-6624-1130-4 (hc)
ISBN 978-1-6624-1129-8 (digital)

Printed in the United States of America

This book is dedicated to the memory of Jerry Brewster, in gratitude for his unwavering generosity. Without him, the compilation of these stories would not have been possible (or even thought of). It was he who inspired us to hunt for these stories, find their true message, and search for our own inner meaning.

Contents

Foreword

It is our intention to share with you a compilation of teaching stories from various traditions, each with its own inner meaning. We have no claim to their originality and believe they are all part of the public domain.

For over fifty years, members of the Brewster Groups have gathered and shared these stories at lunches, dinners, and celebrations. Many have been told and retold in different forms throughout the ages. Often these stories have had a transforming effect on our lives. We hope that the reader will find meaning in these stories and that they touch you as deeply as they have us.

First Get His Attention

A wise man was traveling on a mountain road one day and discovered a merchant in a state of utter frustration. The merchant's stubborn donkey, loaded with heavy bundles, would not budge.

The man shouted and cursed at the creature, but to no avail—the donkey stood steadfast.

After a while, the observant wise man remarked to the merchant, "That's no way to get a donkey to move. You are going about it all wrong. You must encourage him, not curse him. Speak gently to him, and perhaps he will do what you wish."

The merchant glared at his critic. With more than a trace of contempt in his voice, he replied, "I'll tell you what. If you think your method will work, you try it and see where it gets you!"

The wise man agreed. He then picked up a large beam of wood from the side of the road. Returning to the obstinate animal, he struck a powerful blow right between the donkey's eyes.

"Stop! What are you doing?" cried the donkey's astonished owner.

"You said to speak gently to the animal!"

"Yes, of course," answered the wise man, "but first you have to get his attention."

Why We Tell Stories

When the founder of Hasidic Judaism, the great Rabbi Israel Shem Tov, saw misfortune threatening the Jews, it was his custom to go into a certain part of the forest to meditate. There he would light a fire, say a special prayer, and a miracle would be accomplished and the misfortune averted.

Later, when his disciple, the celebrated Maggid of Mezritch, had occasion, for the same reason, to intercede with heaven, he would go to the same place in the forest and say, "Master of the Universe, I do not know how to light the fire, but I am still able to say the prayer," and again a miracle would be accomplished.

Still later, Rabbi Moshe Leib of Sasov, in order to save his people, would go into the forest and say, "I do not know how to light the fire, I do not know the prayer, but I know the place, and this must be sufficient." It was sufficient, and a miracle was accomplished.

Then it fell to Rabbi Israel of Rizhin to overcome misfortune. Sitting in his armchair, his head in his hands, he spoke to God, "I am unable to light the fire, and I do not know the prayer, and I cannot even find the place in the forest. All I can do is to tell the story, and this must be sufficient." And it was.

The Orphan Lion

An orphan lion cub, with his eyes still closed shut from birth, was given milk by a wild ewe who found him in her meadow.

As he grew up, he was adopted by the herd. Running with them, he knew of no other animals. Then one day, a jungle lion roared on a hill. Every lamb and sheep fled, but the little lion looked up. He thought to himself, *How could I have run with sheep for so long?*

The Mansion

A man came to a guru who lived in a great mansion, with long hallways, many flights of stairs, and hundreds of rooms decorated with beautiful paintings and elaborate furniture. The man came to the guru and said, "I wish to be conscious." To this, the guru replied, "I can help you." The guru picked up a spoon, filled it with water, and said, "Take this spoon and carry it through every room of the house without spilling a drop." At first, the man could not even take a few steps without spilling the water, but he persisted. After a few weeks, he was able to walk down a hallway without spilling, but a new obstacle would appear: a stairway, a turn into a room, a piece of furniture in his way, etc... His wish was strong, so he kept trying, and after many years, he was able to accomplish the task given to him. The man came back to the guru and told him of his accomplishment, to which the guru replied, "Take the spoon once again, only this time when you return, describe to me, in detail, the contents of every room."

Complaining

There was once a man who joined a monastery where talking was forbidden. Once every ten years, the monks were allowed to say two words to the abbot. After ten years, the man, now a monk, had his audience with the abbot and said, "Bed hard," and then continued on with his chores. He continued with the hard labors and strict routine of the monastery for another ten years, and when he met with the abbot, he said, "Food terrible," and once again returned to his duties as a monk. Another ten years passed, and once again, it was time to meet with the abbot. He entered the abbot's quarters and said, "I quit!" The abbot replied, "I am not surprised. You've done nothing but complain since you got here."

The Mullah and the Moneylender

    The Mullah's wife scolded him for not having a job, complaining, "If whatever you do is Allah's work, you should see that He pays you!" And so the Mullah, sitting by his window, prayed and asked Allah to pay him one hundred pieces of gold as back pay for all the good work he had done for Him. The Mullah's neighbor, a moneylender, overheard the Mullah's prayers and thought that it would be a chance to teach him a lesson. The moneylender decided to play a trick on him and, as Mullah was praying, threw a bag of money outside his window. The Mullah scooped up the bag! He couldn't believe his eyes. There—there in the bag was his back pay! Once again, the Mullah began to pray, this time thanking Allah for His generosity. A short time later, as Mullah was counting the gold, his wife came in. "Where did you get all of that gold?" she demanded. "It's my back pay from God. I asked Him for it, just as you suggested," replied the Mullah. "There's so much of it!" said his wife. "Yes, I must be a saint,"

answered the Mullah. They began to make plans—new curtains, new furniture, a new outfit for his wife, a new altar for the mosque, new rugs for the prayer room, etc.

The next day, the moneylender sees the Mullah generously tipping a porter, who just delivered a large bundle.

"Mullah, what are you doing? You can't spend that gold. It's mine," he exclaimed.

"Your gold? It's not your gold—God sent it to me. You were merely listening when I asked for it," replied the Mullah.

"Mullah, I threw it down as a joke! You saw me. Now give it back."

"You don't understand," said the Mullah. "You didn't throw it to me—God threw it to me. You were just the vehicle."

"If you don't give me back my money, I will teach you a lesson you will never forget!" said the moneylender.

"I'm sorry, but I will not go against God's will" the Mullah replied.

"In that case, I will take you before the court of summary jurisdiction. I will certainly win, and you will be thrown into prison!" the moneylender threatened.

"You may win," replied the Mullah, "but not because you are right!"

"What? What do you mean?" asked the moneylender.

"Look at me!" the Mullah replied. "The judge will be prejudiced against me because of my appearance. I am in rags. You wear beautiful clothes. I ride an old mule—you ride that fine horse. So you may win, but not because your case is just."

The moneylender, thinking carefully about what the Mullah had just said, answered, "Ha! There is no way you can win this case—no matter what you look like. Here, take my clothes, ride my horse. No matter what you wear or what you ride on, the judge will see that I am right and you will be shown up for the thief that you are."

So, they went in front of the judge. The moneylender, dressed in the Mullah's rags, filed his complaint, telling the judge that the Mullah had his gold and would not return it. The Mullah, very respectfully, asked the judge if they could speak privately in his chambers. This request was granted. When they were in the judge's chambers, the Mullah said, "Your Honor, I must tell you, my neighbor is quite mad. He believes that everything I own is his. That is what this case is really all about."

"That is serious. Can you prove this?" asked the judge.

"Yes," replied the Mullah. "Just ask him who owns the horse I ride. Why, you can even ask him who owns the clothes that I am wearing."

Good Idea

One day the Mullah and his wife were in the village buying goods for the feast to be held that week. He saw a man he had counseled to the faith and who had yet to renounce his infidel ways. He walked up to the man and greeted him with a holy blessing.

"I thank you," the infidel replied. "And how do you fare, good Mullah?"

The Mullah answered him. "I am blessed by Allah with a good wife and many fine children. You can see how Allah blesses the true believers in this land. I see you are still a bachelor, and still an infidel. I am sure that if you took up the true faith, Allah would grant you a wife."

The young man answered, "I am not convinced that getting a wife is enough to make me convert."

The Mullah had perceived that this young man was quite taken with the fairer sex, and so he explained to him; "Mohammed, in his wisdom, decreed that it was Allah's will that a man be allowed to have as many wives as he wishes. I know that your infidel faith does not allow more than one wife."

This impressed the young man. "This is true. I might be persuaded by such an argument."

At this time, the Mullah's wife began to shout after him, calling in a most ungracious way to cease his gossiping and carry her purchases. This caused the infidel to ask, "If you are allowed many wives, why is it that you, a Mullah of great renown, have only one wife?"

"The answer is simple," the Mullah replied. "The prophet said it was allowed to have many wives, but he never said that it was a good idea."

The Shiny Object

The Mullah was working in the fields, preparing the ground for spring planting, when he uncovered something very shiny. He picked it up and looked at it and was shocked to see the image of his dear old grandfather, who had long since passed away. He put the object in his pocket and continued his work.

When he returned home after an extralong day's work, his wife was suspicious of where he had been, especially since she noticed that every few minutes, the Mullah would take something out of his pocket and look at it with loving eyes.

From that time on, day after day, the Mullah would come home late, secretively look at the object lovingly, and put it back in his pocket.

This made her very jealous—she feared that, since her husband had been away from home for so many hours every day, and knowing how lazy he really was, he wasn't really working in the fields but must be having an affair with another woman.

When she could stand it no longer, she waited until the Mullah fell deep asleep and took the object out of his pocket. When she looked at it, all she saw was the image of a wrinkled old woman who vaguely reminded her of her dear old grandmother. She thought to herself, *Ha! If that's who he is chasing after, then I have nothing to worry about.*

Elephant and the Mouse

An elephant met a mouse in the forest. "How is it that you are so small?" spoke the elephant. "Well, you see," said the mouse, "I've been sick."

The Prince Gets Kidnapped

There once was a prince who fell deeply in love with a beautiful princess. After courting her for a year or so, the prince asked for her hand in marriage. She replied that she could not marry him. The prince was perplexed, for he knew she loved him as well, and he asked her why she would not marry him.

The princess explained that she could not marry anyone who did not have a trade, because, she reasoned, the fortunes of life could take away position and power, but knowledge and craftsmanship could never be taken away. Since the prince had idly spent his whole life as the king's heir, he had no skills.

The prince, deeply in love, asked her to wait for him for five years, and he would return to her as a master craftsman. Then they could get married. She readily agreed, hopeful that he would succeed.

The prince decided he would like to learn how to weave carpets. Day after day, month after month, year after year, he diligently applied himself, struggling to learn the intricacies of his chosen craft.

After many failures, producing rugs of awful quality, his work began to gradually improve. Less and less imperfections were found in his carpets. The colors gradually began to find a certain harmony. His patterns slowly started to become pleasing to the eye.

Finally, after five long hard years, the prince had mastered his craft! His tutor could find no difference between his own carpets and the ones made by the prince.

Having kept his promise, the prince set off to claim his bride. But on his way, brigands captured him and held him for ransom. Now the policy in his kingdom was, never give in to kidnappers, no matter who is kidnapped—no ransom would ever be paid.

When the brigands learned that no one would pay the ransom, and fearing for their lives, they decided to kill the prince, since he could identify them. Now the prince, knowing their intentions, pled for his life by explaining to the brigands that he could still be of value to them because he was a master carpet maker and if they would provide him with the proper materials, he would make carpets for them, which could be sold at the local bazaar for a nice profit.

The brigands agreed to spare him his life and provided the prince with the materials he required. After a short time, he produced a magnificent carpet, which the brigands brought to the bazaar for sale.

The prince's tutor, strolling through the marketplace, noticed the rug, recognized the craftsmanship, and deciphered a message woven into the carpet. The message read, "Help, I have been kidnapped and am being held captive in the basement of such and such place."

The prince was rescued, the brigands were put in jail, and the princess and prince were married.

Butter Side Up

One morning, in the town of Chelm, a place where the people see and do things a little differently than anywhere else, Schlomo, the town klutz, was buttering his bread before sitting down to his breakfast. Of course, being who he was, Schlomo accidentally dropped the buttered bread. It fell to the floor.

Now, everyone who has ever dropped a piece of buttered bread knows that it always falls butter side down. Not this time, this time the bread landed butter side up! Schlomo was amazed at his good fortune and bent down to pick it up. As he straightened up and started toward the table, he tripped, and once again, he dropped the bread. Looking down, he saw that the bread had landed butter side up again! How could this be? He decided to bring the bread to the rabbi, the wisest man in the whole town of Chelm, to ask him to explain this miracle.

Picking up the bread, Schlomo grabbed his hat and coat (twice dropping the bread, which continued to land butter side up) and headed out the door. On his way, being the klutz that he was, Schlomo dropped the bread several more times, and miraculously, it always landed butter side up!

Rushing in to the rabbi's study, Schlomo excitedly explained to the rabbi what had occurred and, as if to demonstrate, accidentally tripped on the rug and dropped the bread.

Once again, the piece of bread landed butter side up!

The rabbi, upon hearing Schlomo's story and witnessing this miracle himself, sat in deep contemplation for a very long time, trying to understand the reason that this particular piece of buttered bread would always land buttered side up.

Finally, he rose and said, "I have the explanation! It is obvious that you buttered the bread on the wrong side!"

The Mullah's Donkey

A neighbor knocked on the Mullah's door and asked, "Can I borrow your donkey?" The donkey was in the barn, but the Mullah did not want to lend him the animal, so the Mullah replied, "No, my cousin borrowed the donkey earlier today." Just then, by coincidence, the donkey brayed. "But, Mullah," the neighbor objected, "you just said you loaned him to your cousin." The Mullah insisted, "Who are you going to listen to, me or a donkey?"

Look Who Thinks He's Nothing

A beggar, exhausted after a day and a half of fruitless begging, came to a temple in a small village and went in to rest. Picking a dim spot in the corner near the altar, he sat quietly and rested his weary body.

After some time had passed and the beggar was getting ready to leave, the head of the village came in, knelt before the altar, and began to pray: "Lord, I know I am nothing, but I need Your help. Our village is facing many problems. I am insignificant. It is Your voice that must act through me. O Lord, please help us in this time of need." The village head then got up and sat in one of the seats near the altar.

At this moment, the banker of the village entered. He also knelt before the altar and prayed: "God, now is the time for Your mercy to fall upon us. We will be facing difficult times ahead, and I know that even though I will do all I can, I am really nothing, that it is not me but You that will act in me. I know You will not desert us." He then arose and sat next to the village head.

The beggar, watching and hearing all this, was touched by their selfless prayers and was himself moved to pray. The beggar rose from his feet and walked forward. Falling to his knees in front of the altar, he cried out, "Lord, I know I am nothing." Hearing this, the village head, smiling smugly, nudged the banker with his elbow, saying, "Ha! Look who thinks he's nothing!"

Smuggling

The Mullah would cross the border every day with his donkey loaded with straw. The guards, who knew he was smuggling something across the border, would carefully inspect the donkey and its load, finding nothing. Clearly the Mullah was becoming more and more prosperous. The guards were baffled. Years later, the Mullah met one of the guards, who had been retired for a long time, in a coffee shop. The guard said, "I'm not a guard anymore, and I can no longer prosecute you, but I knew you were smuggling something. We could never find any contraband. Please, tell an old man, what were you smuggling?" To this, the Mullah replied, "Donkeys!"

Good Swimmer?

In the old days, men were permitted to have more than one wife. Mullah himself took a second wife, who was younger than the first one. One evening, he came home to find them quarreling about which of them Mullah loved more. At first, Mullah told them he loved them both, but neither of them was satisfied with his answer. Then the older one asked, "Well, just suppose the three of us were in a boat and it started to sink. Which of us would you try to save?" Mullah thought for a moment and then said to his older wife, "My dear, you know how to swim, don't you?"

You Are Right

Hodja was once a judge. One day, a man came to his house to complain about his neighbor. Hodja listened carefully and then said to him, "You know, you are right." The man went away happily.

A little while later, the first man's neighbor came to see Hodja. He complained about the first man. Hodja listened carefully to him too and then said, "You know, you are right."

Hodja's wife had been listening to all this, and when the second man left, she turned to Hodja and said, "Hodja, you told both men they were right. That's impossible. They both can't be right."

Hodja listened carefully to his wife and then said to her, "You know, my dear, you are right."

Sufi Prayer

There is an old Sufi prayer that goes like this: "O God, why is it that You are always so close to me, while I am always so far from You."

One of a Thousand

Of the thousand that hear about the true path, only one understands its true significance.

Of the thousand that understand its true significance, only one considers following it.

Of the thousand that consider following it, only one actually steps and walks on the path, beginning the journey.

Of the thousand who begin the journey, only one, upon reaching the first crossroads, makes the right choice.

Of the thousand who reach the first crossroads and makes the right choice, only one...and so on, and so on, and so on...

It Is Said

It is said, Buddha pointed the way to enlightenment,
and everyone looked at his finger.

Payment at the Turkish Bath

One day Mullah went to a Turkish bath, but as he was dressed so poorly, the attendants didn't pay much attention to him. They gave him only a scrap of soap, a rag for a loincloth, and an old towel. When Mullah left, he gave each of the two attendants a gold coin. Both attendants were astonished as he had not complained about their poor service. They wondered if they had treated him better whether he would have given them an even larger tip.

The next week, Mullah came again. This time, they treated him like royalty and gave him embroidered towels and a loincloth of silk. After being massaged and perfumed, he left the bath, handing each attendant the smallest copper coin possible. When the attendants protested in confusion about the last tip and this one, Mullah answered, "I see you don't understand. Well, this copper coin is for my last visit. The gold coins were meant for today's."

Big Pot Died

On one occasion, Hodja borrowed a big pot from his neighbor. When Hodja returned the pot, the neighbor saw that there was a smaller cooking pot inside of it. He asked, "Hodja, where did this smaller pot come from?"

"Apparently the large one had been pregnant and gave birth to this small pot," Hodja replied. The neighbor, without thinking, accepted both pots.

Some weeks later, Hodja needed to borrow the same large pot. The neighbor, only too happy to oblige, lent it to him once again.

A month passed by, and the neighbor, wanting his pot returned, called on Hodja to ask him for it. Hodja, with a concerned look, replied sadly, "I am sorry to tell you this, but your big pot died." The neighbor, at first, was puzzled, then he inquired angrily, "How could it die? It was only a pot."

"If you believe that the pot could have given birth, why won't you believe that it could die?" quipped Hodja.

How Do You Know?

In ancient China, there was a farmer without a son. As you know, there is a great value in having sons in China even today—well, back then, it was even more so. The farmer's friends in the village would commiserate with him about his bad fortune, to which he would look at them soberly and reply, "How do you know it is bad?"

After a few years, his wife gave birth to a son. The villagers all came over to celebrate his good fortune. Once again, he posed the question, "How do you know it is good?"

The boy, now seven or eight years old, was running through the fields and accidentally stepped into a ditch and broke his leg. In those days, a broken leg meant you would be lame for the rest of your life because the healers did not have the skills they have now. The villagers, on hearing the news, came over to commiserate with the farmer on his bad fortune. He asked them again, "How do you know it is bad?"

Now the boy is seventeen, and a war breaks out all over the land. A great warlord comes marching through the village and takes all the young men into his army, but they don't take the farmer's son because he is lame. "How do you know it is good?" etc…

Mustard Seed

One day when Buddha was relating his teaching to his disciples, a woman came to him who could not accept her baby's death. She carried the dead baby's body with her always. Showing his corpse to the Buddha, she asked sorrowfully, "Since you are a great saint, would you perform a miracle and bring my baby to life?"

"Certainly," the Buddha replied, "but in order to do so, I'll need some help from you. I will need you to find me a mustard seed from a house that has never known death."

The woman went from house to house in the village, becoming more and more frustrated in her search to find this special seed. After several days' search, she began to realize that there was no one who had escaped the touch of death. With this realization, the woman buried her baby's body and became a disciple of Buddha. As the Buddha had promised, the miracle was performed. It wasn't the baby, however, but the woman who was brought back to life.

The Thief and the Moon

Ryoken, a Zen priest, lived in solitude and poverty. Late one evening, as he was meditating under a full moon, a thief snuck into the hut and took his few possessions: a rice bowl and a spoon. As the thief began to sneak away, the monk said, "Don't forget the cloak behind the door. It is very valuable." The thief, unaware of the monk's presence, was startled. He hesitated, then looked behind the door, took the cloak, and scurried away. After the thief was gone, the monk thought to himself, *If only I could have given him this moon.*

The Mantra

A king decided to visit his minister of state. On arriving at his house, the king was informed that the minister was meditating and had left instructions not to be disturbed under any conditions. After a short while, the minister came into the room and apologized to the king for keeping him waiting. "You see, my guru gave me a special mantra today," the minister told the king. The king, impressed with the glowing look on the minister's face and the sense of inner peace he was radiating, asked the minister to give him the mantra.

"I cannot," replied the minister. "Only my guru has the authority to give you this mantra. If I gave it to you, you would not get the same results."

"That doesn't make sense," said the king, "You know the mantra, so I can't see why, if you give it to me, I would not get the same results."

"I'm sorry, I cannot," replied the minister.

"I insist," said the king in an angry voice.

The minister thought for a few moments and then shouted to the guards, "The king is impertinent! Arrest him at once!" The guards did not move. The minister again shouted, "Guards, arrest the king!" Again the guards stood their ground. One more time, the minister ordered the guards to arrest the king.

The king, who was growing angrier and angrier, shouted, "I'll show you who's impertinent! Guards, arrest the minister." The guards surrounded the minister and took him into their custody.

As they began to lead him away, the minister smiled and said to the king, "You see, no matter how many times I asked them to arrest you, they would not, because I do not have that authority. Yet one word from you, and it was done. It is exactly the same with the mantra."

Fasting

A disciple asked his superior why it was that their guru did not believe that extended fasting was spiritually beneficial. The superior replied that their guru had said that mortification of the body not only weakened it but could also interfere with the kind of intense meditation that they practiced; the disciple pointed out that he had heard that their guru had actually fasted when he was younger and asked if that was true. "Yes," answered the superior. "But let me give you an example of the kind of fasting he did. Once when our guru went into seclusion in order to meditate for six days, he took a bag filled with six loaves of bread to provide him with sustenance. When the six days were finished and he picked up the bag in which he had brought the loaves, he was surprised to find it so heavy. When he looked inside, he saw that the six loaves of bread were still there. This kind of fasting is always allowed.

Donkey's Choice

A wise man asked his donkey, "On which path do you enjoy riding the best, the one going uphill or the one going downhill?"

"I like neither," replied the donkey. "Whatever happened to riding the straight path?"

"With this attitude," the wise man answered, "you will remain a donkey for eternity. In this life, the straight path can only take you so far."

The King Spoke to Me

Nasrudin returned to his village from the imperial capital, and the villagers gathered around to hear what had passed. "At this time," said Nasrudin, "I only want to say that the king spoke to me." All the villagers but the simplest ran off to spread the wonderful news. The remaining villager asked, "What did the king say to you?"

"What he said—and quite distinctly, for everyone to hear—was...'Get out of my way!'"

The Sinner

A monk went to his teacher one day and said, "Last night I realized, with great regret, I must leave the order. Recently I've thought about my life and came to the conclusion that, since I am in my heart a great sinner, there is really no hope for me to attain enlightenment, and so I feel it's useless for me to go on."

The teacher smiled and replied, "Don't you know, a saint is nothing more than a sinner who never stopped trying."

No One Lies

It is written that, to a Taoist monk, everyone tells the truth. For example, when asking two thirty-nine-year-old women their ages, the first replied, "Thirty-nine," and the second, "Twenty-nine."

To the monk, they both said the truth: the first told him her age; the second told him, "I'm afraid of growing old."

Two Mice

One night, two mice were playing on the rafters in a barn. They became so engaged in their game that, in their carelessness, they both toppled off the rafter and fell into a large bucket filled with milk. Desperately they swam around and around until both began to realize that their situation was hopeless.

At this point, one of the mice gave up. Gasping with his last breath, he said, "It's useless to keep on swimming. We have no chance to escape." He then stopped struggling, sank, and drowned. The other mouse kept swimming until he was so completely exhausted that, finally, with one last stroke, he passed out. Later, he awoke to find himself lying on top of a bucket of freshly churned butter.

Unanswerable Question

"There is nothing which cannot be answered by means of my doctrine," said a monk, in the teahouse where Nasrudin sat.

"And yet just a short time ago, I was challenged by a scholar with an unanswerable question," said Nasrudin.

"I could have answered it if I had been there."

"Very well. He asked, 'Why are you breaking into my house in the middle of the night?'"

Chasing Enlightenment

One of the monks in a monastery was well-known for his extreme zealousness and effort. Day and night, he would sit in meditation, and days would pass before he would eat or sleep. As time passed, he grew thinner and more and more exhausted. During meditation, he often nearly drifted off to sleep. The master finally asked him to slow down, but the monk refused to take the master's advice and even drove himself harder.

Finally, the master asked him, "Why are you rushing so?" The monk replied. "There is no time to waste."

"How do you know," asked the master, "that enlightenment is running on in front of you so that you have to run after it? It might be that enlightenment is coming up from behind you and all you need to encounter it is just to stand still. If that is true, you are actually running away from it."

Were My Prayers Valid?

A farmer, who was a very devout man and who had never missed Sabbath services, was trapped at home by a raging snowstorm. There was nothing the farmer could do; the roads were impassable. The next day, upon arriving at the synagogue, the farmer confessed to the rabbi that, not knowing the prayers, he had instead recited the alphabet over and over, asking God to arrange the letters in their proper order. "Were my prayers valid, or did I sin?" he asked the rabbi. "Not only did you not sin," the rabbi replied, "but last night your prayers were more sincere than mine."

All Men Are Dead

All men are dead except
those that follow the true path.

All those that follow the true path are dead
except those that know.

All those that know are dead
except those that practice.

All those who practice are dead
except those who practice with righteous intention.

And all those who practice with righteous intention
are in very grave danger.

Dand'l Noim
Twelfth-century Egyptian Sufi

Forgive My Sins

For many years, a monk continually prayed to God, "Lord, when will you forgive me my sins?" For years, this was the basis of all his prayers. Over and over, he repeated this prayer: "O Lord, when will you forgive my sins?" One day, after praying for many hours, he heard the voice of God reverberate through the room, "I will forgive you your sins when you stop committing them."

Anybody Else?

A man was being chased by a tiger. He came to the edge of a cliff and went over the side. As he was falling, he grabbed on to a branch and held on for his life. After the tiger had lost interest and left, the man began to scream, "Help! Is there anybody up there? Is there anybody up there?" over and over again.

Finally, he heard a booming voice coming from the heavens say, "Have faith and let go of the branch."

"Is there anybody else?" shouted the man.

I Had a Donkey Like That

The Mullah had just purchased a large tract of land with a nice-sized house and invited his very wealthy friend for a visit so he could show off proudly his new digs. After showing off the house, he brought his guest out to the backyard to gaze at the expanse of the Mullah's property.

His friend asked, "How far does your property extend?" To which the Mullah puffed proudly, "Do you see that fig tree all the way over there on the left?" He pointed.

"Yes," answered his friend.

"And do you see that date tree all the way over there to the right?" he asked proudly.

"Yes," his friend answered again.

"Well, all of that, and in between, is mine!"

"Very nice," his friend responded, "but if I got on my donkey early in the morning on one side of my property, I would not be able to reach the other side by nightfall."

Without batting an eye, the Mullah commiserated, "I once had a donkey like that."

Sandals

One day, Nasrudin was taking a walk in his village, when several of his neighbors approached him. "Nasrudin Hodja!" they said to him. "You are so wise and holy! Please take us as your pupils to teach us how we should live our lives and what we should do!" Nasrudin paused then said, "Alright, I will teach you the first lesson right now. The most important thing is to take very good care of your feet and sandals. You must keep them clean and neat at all times."

The neighbors listened attentively until they glanced down at his feet, which were in fact quite dirty and shod in old sandals that seemed about to fall apart. "But, Hodja," said one of them, "your feet are terribly dirty, and your sandals are a mess! How do you expect us to follow your teachings if you don't carry them out yourself?"

"Well," replied Nasrudin, "I don't go around asking people how I should live my life either, do I?"

Father Sebastian

There was a flood warning. Everyone needed to evacuate the town. One of the villagers went to the church in order to take Father Sebastian, known all over as a man of great faith, to higher ground and safety. The father refused, saying, "Don't worry about me. Save yourself. I have faith. The Lord will provide." Father Sebastian continued offering his prayers.

The rains came. The town began to flood. A second villager came by in his boat and saw Father Sebastian on the steps of the church praying to his Lord. "Father, get in my boat, and I will take you to safety," cried the villager. "No, my son, I am in good hands. I have faith. The Lord will take care of me. Go save yourself," he responded. The villager, not knowing what else to do, and in fear for his own safety, steered his boat away toward safety.

A little later, as the storm grew worse and the floods had risen to the church doors, another boat came by. The villager, upon seeing Father Sebastian praying at the doorway, called to him and pled with him to get in the boat and be taken to safety. Once again, the father, proclaiming his faith, assured the villager that he would be fine. Surely the Lord would not forsake a man with such unbending faith. The villager, not knowing what else to do, left him at the church and sped away to a safe haven.

Now the floods were up to the roof of the church. Father Sebastian was still praying and proclaiming his faith (this time on the roof). Once again, a villager in a boat came by and implored the father to get in his boat. Once again, despite the villager's protestations, Father Sebastian refused, saying, "I insist you save yourself in your way. I have no fear. God will not let me die." The villager had no choice and rowed away.

The floodwaters continued to rise, and sure enough, Father Sebastian was pulled into the waters and drowned.

Appearing at the holy gates, the father said to St. Peter, "I don't understand. I prayed. I had such faith. How could God have let me drown?"

"Let you drown?" replied St. Peter. "He sent you three boats!"

The Lost Fellow

The great rebbe of Chelm was taking a leisurely stroll along the riverbank when he came upon a group of travelers who had just crossed the river by ferry. The travelers were all moaning and crying, bewailing the fact that they lost one of their companions in the river, believing he must have drowned.

The rebbe asked, "What makes you think one of you is missing?"

One of the travelers replied, "When we boarded the ferry, we were ten," showing the rebbe ten ferry ticket stubs, "but now we're only nine—look…" And the man counted one of his companions, pointing to each, as he counted. "See? One, two, three, four, five, six, seven, eight, nine." And another traveler said, "That's our problem. One is missing," and he recounted each of his fellows. "One, two, three, four, five, six, seven, eight, nine."

The rebbe pondered on this for quite a while, as was his custom when presented with a difficult problem. After an unusually long time, the rebbe said, "Well, you know, I think I can return your lost fellow."

They said, "How could you do that?"

He said, "I have certain powers. I believe I can return your lost fellow."

They said, "If you can do that, we will certainly be in your debt."

"Okay." He said, "Now, give me the ticket stubs and stand over there," and he lined up each traveler side by side. He then counted the stubs. "One, two, three, four, five, six, seven, eight, nine, ten."

The rebbe then gave each traveler one ticket stub and said, "There, you see, since there are ten ticket stubs and each one of you is holding one of them, you are once again ten companions."

Turban of Wisdom

One day an illiterate neighbor brought Hodja a badly scribbled letter to read for him. When Hodja complained that it was illegible, the man accused him of being unworthy of the turban of wisdom that he wore. Hodja was furious at the insult and slammed the turban on his neighbor's head. "Here," he shouted, "you wear it and see if you can read the letter!"

Without a Recipe

Nasrudin was carrying home a piece of liver and the recipe for liver pie. Suddenly, a bird of prey swooped down and snatched the piece of meat from his hand. As the bird flew off, Nasrudin called after it, "Foolish bird! You have the liver, but what can you do with it without the recipe?"

The Parking Spot

Moishe was driving around in circles, looking for a parking spot. After about half an hour, frustrated because he could not find a place to put his car, he looked up to the heavens and said, "Lord, I know I haven't been a good Jew, but I promise I will change my ways. I will keep the Sabbath, give money to the poor, I will even keep kosher, if you help me find a parking spot." Before the last words were out of his mouth, miraculously, a spot appeared right in front of the place he wished to go. Without batting an eye, Moishe looked up and said, "Forget it, I found one already!"

I Hid It Under Your Pillow

In India, many years ago, a merchant who had just completed a lucrative business deal, started on his way home. As he walked, he counted his money and was pleased with the amount. After some distance, he was joined by another merchant who said that since there were brigands in the area; it would be in both their interests if they traveled together. The first merchant readily agreed, not knowing that the second merchant had been following him for a long time, and was really a thief who had seen the merchant counting his money. They continued on their journey together, and when the sun began to dip below the horizon, they came upon an inn where they could spend the night. The thief suggested that they share a room. It would be cheaper, he reasoned, and they could keep each other company. The merchant agreed again, and after dinner, both men exhausted from their journey, immediately retired. In the morning, the thief observed the merchant very carefully, and when the merchant left the room to take his bath, the thief proceeded to search the merchant's bags. Finding nothing, he began to look everywhere: under the merchant's mattress, through his clothing, under his pillow. But he could not find the money.

Later, after having breakfast, they continued on their journey. Again, in the evening, they stopped at a local inn, and when morning came, the same scenario took place. When the merchant had left the room, naked save for a towel wrapped around his waist, the thief searched through the merchant's bags, through his clothing, under his pillow, under the mattress, and so on. Again he couldn't find the money. It began to drive him crazy. He thought of the sight of the merchant counting his money at the side of the road. *It must be somewhere*, the thief thought to himself.

Once again, they traveled all day, and that evening, they came to the merchant's house. As they were saying goodbye, the thief broke down and confessed that he was not really a merchant but a thief and that his intention in traveling with him was to rob him of his money. "You drove me crazy," said the thief. "I looked everywhere, in your bags, through your clothes, under your pillow, under the mattress. I searched everywhere I could think of, and I still couldn't find the money. Tell me where you hid it, and I promise you, I will never steal again."

"All right," said the merchant, "if you really promise to never steal again, I'll tell you. I hid it under your pillow."

Dharma Battle

Kosen, a famous monk in ancient Japan, was coming to a certain monastery and wished to do dharma battle upon his arrival. After much deliberation, the monks decided to send Aka, a half-blind novice, to ensure a loss. Kosen would then honor the monastery by staying there for a night, as was the custom in those parts. Unfortunately, their plans went awry, and Aka, unbelievably, won the battle. After losing and praising the monastery for being at such a high level that a mere novice could have beaten him, Kosen told the head monk that he could not stay.

The head monk, stunned, asked Kosen to relate what had happened. Kosen, in reply, said, "I started the battle by holding up one finger—signifying that all is Buddha. He held up two fingers, indicating that there is Buddha and also his followers.

"I then held up three fingers, indicating that yes, there is Buddha and his followers, but they must live the dharma. With this, I thought I had won the battle, but he then held up his closed hand, revealing that all three are actually one. This clearly defeated me, so you see, I must go on."

Sadly, the head monk bid Kosen goodbye. After he had gone, the monk called Aka and asked him to tell him of the battle. Aka replied, "The nerve of that man! Would you believe that the first thing he did was insult me by holding up one finger, indicating that I only had one eye? But since I was given this responsibility, I tried not to get angry and held up two fingers, indicating that he had two eyes. And do you know what that idiot did? He held up three fingers, indicating that between us, we had three eyes! At that point, I could no longer control myself. I got so angry that I raised my fist to hit him, but the coward turned and walked away."

Hark, I Hear the Cannons Roar

The Mullah was in a café bragging about what a great actor he was, going on and on, explaining to anyone who would listen that he was the best actor in the world. Finally, a man came up to him and asked if he could really act. The Mullah unabashedly expounded all of his talents and assured him that he really could act. The man, looking at his watch, said that there was just barely enough time and, if the Mullah was willing to go to the city right away, he would get his big break. The Mullah eagerly agreed. The man told him all the arrangements had been made and to get in the cab waiting outside. As the Mullah was entering the cab, the man told him that he had only one line and to be prepared, as there was just enough time for him to get to the theater before he would get onstage. His line was "Hark, I hear the cannons roar." No sooner had the cab door closed than it started to speed away. During the cab ride, the Mullah began to rehearse his line, trying to find the best delivery. Over and over, he repeated, "HARK, I hear the cannons roar," stressing first one than another syllable. "Hark, I hear the cannons roar," "Hark, I HEAR the cannons roar," "Hark, I hear THE cannons roar," "Hark, I hear the CANNONS roar," etc. The cab pulled up to the train station. Another man approached the cab and asked if the Mullah was the actor that was expected. As the Mullah nodded yes, the man, in great haste, pulled him out of the cab and rushed him onto the train. Just as the Mullah entered the train, the doors shut and it began its way into the city.

Once again, as he settled into his seat, the Mullah began to rehearse his line, trying to find the perfect delivery. "Hark, I hear the cannons ROAR," "Hark, I HEAR the cannons roar," "Hark, I hear THE cannons roar," "Hark, I hear the CANNONS roar," etc. Over, and over, and over, again, and again, and again…

Finally, he felt ready! He had mastered the line and found the perfect delivery! The train arrived at the station.

A man rushed the Mullah from the train into yet another cab, telling him that there was just enough time to get to the theater. As before, the Mullah, once seated in the cab, rehearsed, "Hark, I hear the cannons ROAR," "HARK, I hear the cannons roar," "Hark, I HEAR the cannons roar," "Hark, I hear THE cannons roar," etc.

The cabbie, screeching his brakes, stopped at the backstage entryway to the theater. Another man was anxiously waiting for him, grabbed him, and while rushing him to the stage, asked if he knew his line. The Mullah nodded yes and was thrown onto the stage. At that very same moment, there was a loud boom!

The Mullah, taken aback, turned and looked up and said, "What the hell was that?"

Cat Tale

One day Mullah bought three pounds of meat and took it home to his wife. Then he returned to work. Immediately, his wife called her friends and prepared a superb luncheon.

In the evening, Mullah returned for supper, and his wife offered him nothing but bread and onions. He turned to her and said, "But why haven't you prepared anything from the meat?"

"I rinsed the meat and was going to put it on the stove when this damn cat came up and took it away," she said.

Mullah at once ran to get the scales. Then he found the cat and weighed it. It was exactly three pounds! Then he turned to his wife and said, "Look here! If what I have just weighed is the cat, then where's the meat? But if this is the meat, then where's the cat?"

The Lottery

A guy named Joe found himself in dire trouble. His business had gone bust, and he was in serious financial trouble. He was so desperate that he decided to ask God for help. He began to pray: "God, please help me. I've lost my business, and if I don't get some money, I'm going to lose my house as well. Please let me win the lottery."

Lottery night came, and somebody else won. Joe again prayed: "God, please let me win the lottery! I've lost my business, my house, and I'm going to lose my car as well." Lottery night came, and Joe still had no luck. Once again, he prayed: "My God, why have you forsaken me? I've lost my business, my house, and my car. My wife and children are starving. I don't often ask You for help, and I have always been a good servant to You. *Please* just let me win the lotto this one time so I can get my life back in order."

Suddenly there was a blinding flash of light as the heavens opened, and Joe was confronted by the voice of God Himself: "JOE, MEET ME HALFWAY ON THIS ONE... BUY A TICKET!"

Finding God

A monk traveled through the mountains to meet a famous guru. After several days of waiting, was able to arrange a meeting with him. The guru asked him why he came; what was his question? The man replied, "I have been searching for God for many years without any results. I have heard from many sources that you know the way to him. Will you help me?"

"So, you want to find God. Well, if what you say is true and you really wish to struggle, I will do all I can to help you," replied the guru. He stared at the monk for a long time and then said, "You will have to go and live in the desert for one year. I will give you certain exercises that you must practice every day without fail. But I warn you, they are very difficult. Are you willing to do this?"

"If they will help me find God, I will not fail to do them," replied the seeker. He then received instructions and went into the desert.

After one year, he returned to the guru. "Did you find God?" asked the guru.

"No," replied the monk, "I did all the exercises faithfully, but He still eludes me."

"Well," said the guru, "your search will take longer for you than I thought." The guru thought for a moment. "Look, do you see that mountain over there?" he said, pointing to a very high peak in the distance. "At the top, there is a cave with a very special atmosphere. Certain monks have become enlightened there, leaving a fine vibration that will be of help to you in your quest. You must live in that cave for two years practicing certain prayers and exercises, which I will now show you.

"You must do these exercises every four hours, day and night, during your retreat. Will you agree to this?"

"If it will help me find God, I will do as you ask," replied the monk. After searching the lonely mountain terrain, the monk found the cave. He began practicing the prayers and exercises the guru had given him, all the while enveloped in the special atmosphere which the previous monks had left. The two years finally passed, and again the monk returned and sat at the feet of his teacher. "Did you find what you were searching for?" asked the guru. "Again I've failed," replied the monk despondently. "I think there is no hope for me."

"Come with me," said the teacher and led the monk to the side of a nearby river.

"Kneel down on the bank with your head close to the water," the monk complied. Suddenly the guru seized the monk's head with both of his hands and thrust it beneath the water and held it fast. Seconds passed, then minutes, the monk began to thrash violently. Finally, just as the monk could hold his breath no longer, the guru pulled him out of the water and asked, "A second ago, while your head was in the water, what did you wish for?"

"More than anything in the world, I wished for a breath of air," replied the monk. "Well then, when you want to find God with that kind of wish, you won't have to find Him, He will find you."

The Banyan Tree

An itinerant monk sat warming himself by a fire one night. A beggar approached and asked if he could share the fire's warmth for a little while. The monk not only agreed but also gave him half his dinner and invited him to spend the night. The monk unrolled a sleeping mat on the ground for the beggar; for himself, he used his worn blanket.

The next morning, the monk insisted the beggar eat his last remaining food, whereupon the latter transformed into the god Shiva. To the monk, Shiva said, "As you have been so kind to me, I will grant you one wish." Overwhelmed, the monk asked, "Would you answer any question that I ask?"

"Anything you like," replied Shiva.

The monk became very still, looked inwardly, and asked, "I would like to know how long it will take me to achieve enlightenment."

Slowly Shiva looked around, then he pointed to a large, spreading banyan tree, crowned with tens of thousands of leaves. "If every leaf on that tree represents a lifetime, that's how long it will take you to achieve enlightenment," he replied sadly.

Hearing this, the monk fell to his knees in prostration and wept tears of joy. He thanked Shiva for delivering such wonderful news.

With astonishment, Shiva said, "I don't understand! Until now each time I've answered that question, the asker leaves devastated. Why are you so happy?"

The monk looked up at Shiva with a glowing face and replied, "For such a precious thing, such a short amount of time!"

Two Monks Walking

Two monks were walking through the woods when they came upon a shallow river. At the riverbed, there was a beautiful young woman who wished to cross but could not manage the currents. Now the monks, according to their custom, were strictly not allowed to have any physical contact with women. Upon seeing the woman's predicament, the older monk picked her up, carried her across the river, gently placed her down on the other side, and continued on his way. The younger monk watched in amazement.

After traveling through the forest for a few more hours, the younger monk, who could no longer contain himself, asked the elder, "How could you have carried that woman across the river when you know we are forbidden to have any contact with women?" Calmly the older monk responded, "I left the woman back at the river. Why are you still carrying her?"

With All My Heart

While journeying along the back roads of Poona, in India, a monk met Krishna.

Immediately recognizing him and after receiving permission to ask a question, he said, "Krishna, if I loved you with all my heart, how many incarnations will it take me to reach enlightenment?"

Krishna looked at him, in him, and through him. He weighed his future and his past and said, "If you loved me with all your heart, it will take you seven incarnations to reach enlightenment."

The monk then asked, "If instead of loving you, I hated you with all my heart, how many more incarnations will it take me then?"

"Then it would take only three," Krishna replied.

"But I don't understand, why would it be shorter?" asked the monk.

"Because, if you hated me with all your heart," replied Krishna, "you would always have me in your heart."

Smoking

In a monastery one evening, two monks sat quietly smoking. One monk suddenly looked at the other monk and said, "Do you think it is right for us to be sitting here, smoking during meditation?"

"I don't know," said the second monk. "Why don't you ask your superior and I'll ask mine?" They agreed, and the next day, the first monk arrived to see the second monk sitting there smoking as before.

"How can you smoke?" he remarked. "I asked my superior if it was all right to smoke while meditating, and he said absolutely not."

"That's interesting," answered the second monk. "I asked mine if it was all right to meditate while smoking, and he said, 'Absolutely. Meditate every chance you get!'"

Asking Questions

The Buddha said, "When I first came, you asked certain questions which I was not ready to answer, so I remained silent. Now that you are ready to hear these truths and I am ready to answer, no one asks."

Woodcutter in the Sahara

The forester was rather surprised to see such an unlikely figure as Nasrudin applying for a job.

"I'll give you a chance," he said, "although you don't look the type who could fell trees. Take this axe and chop down as many trees as you can from that plantation."

After three days, Nasrudin reported to him.

"How many trees have you felled?"

"All the trees in the plantation."

The forester looked, and sure enough, there were no trees left. Nasrudin had done as much work as would be expected from thirty men.

"But where did you learn to chop trees at that rate?"

"In the Sahara Desert."

"But there aren't any trees in the Sahara!"

"There aren't any now!" said Nasrudin.

Whatever You Say

One day, the king invited Mullah to his palace for dinner. The royal chef prepared, among other dishes, a cabbage recipe for the occasion.

After the dinner, the king asked, "How did you like the cabbage?"

"It was very delicious," complimented Mullah.

"I thought it tasted awful," said the king.

"You're right," added Mullah, "it was very bland."

"But you just said it tasted delicious," the king noted.

"Yes, but I'm the servant of His Majesty, not of the cabbage," he replied.

Make the People Stop Talking

One day, Mullah and his son went on a journey. Mullah preferred to let his son ride the donkey while he walked. Along the way, they passed some travelers. "Look at that healthy young boy on the donkey! That's today's youth for you! They have no respect for their elders! He rides while his poor father walks!" The words made the lad feel very ashamed, and he insisted that his father ride while he walked.

So Mullah climbed on the donkey, and the boy walked by his side.

Soon they met another group. "Well, look at that! Poor little boy has to walk while his father rides the donkey," they exclaimed. This time, Mullah climbed onto the donkey behind his son.

Soon they met another group, who said, "Look at that poor donkey! He has to carry the weight of two people." Mullah then told his son, "The best thing is for both of us to walk. Then no one can complain." So they continued their journey on foot. Again they met some travelers. "Just look at those fools. Both of them are walking under this hot sun, and neither of them is riding the donkey!" In exasperation, Mullah lifted the donkey onto his shoulders and said, "Come on, if we don't do this, it will be impossible to make people stop talking."

Rabbi Zusya's Deathbed

Rabbi Zusya, a wise and venerable old man, was lying on his deathbed surrounded by his family and disciples, when he suddenly sat straight up in his bed and said, "I just had a vision in which I visited the world beyond this one and met with the great sages and saints from the past.

"They did not ask me, 'Zusya, why were you not more like Moses in your life?' Their question was, 'Zusya, why were you not more like Zusya in your life?'"

The Monk and the Snake

A monk was traveling the back roads of India when he came to a small village where he decided to spend the night. The villagers were very hospitable and generously offered him food and drink, as well as a comfortable place to sleep. The next morning, as he was getting ready to leave, he walked around the village and saw how poor they were. He realized what a sacrifice it was for them to have fed him so lavishly and said to them, "I am a really a great magician, and since you were so kind to me, I will grant you any wish, if it is within my powers to do so."

The people of the village were overjoyed to hear this. They told the magician that a large and malevolent snake was, at that time, biting many people and generally terrorizing the village.

"Please, great master," they asked, "stop the snake from biting us so that we can walk peacefully through our village."

"Easily done," the master said and went off in search of the snake.

Finding the snake resting under a large sunny date palm, the master said, "You know I have power over all forms of life and you must do my bidding."

"Yes," said the snake. "What is it you wish of me?"

"From now on," said the master, "you are not to bite the people of this village. Will you take this vow?"

"Yes," answered the snake, "I promise."

The master went on with his travels and, about a year later, found himself in the same vicinity. Remembering the village and recalling how kind they were, he returned and again spent the night there. The following morning, he asked the villagers if their problem with the snake had been resolved.

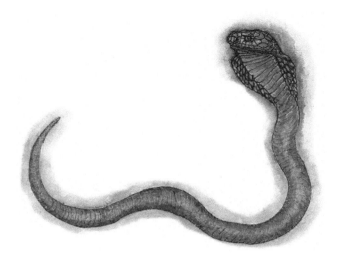

The villagers laughed and said that since his last visit there, everything was fine. Before the master left, he decided to visit the snake and see how it was faring.

After a long search, the master could find no sign of it. As he was just about to give up, he heard a sound coming from behind a rock. He looked and found the snake cowering there. The snake was now a shadow of its former self. Bruised and beaten, he looked as if he was almost at the point of death. "How did you get into this terrible state?" asked the master. "You asked me not to bite the villagers," replied the snake. "But now they are no longer afraid of me! And worse, whenever they see me, they throw stones at me and beat me with their clubs. All I can do now is hide."

"You fool!" said the master. "I ordered you not to bite them, but I never told you not to hiss at them."

Fish in the Ocean

A disciple visited his guru and said, "I have searched for God in many ways. I have practiced many exercises and have offered many prayers, but I still have not found God. Can you tell me where He is?"

"I can no more tell you how to find God," replied the guru, "than I can tell a fish how to find the ocean."

Good or Bad?

One day, Hodja's apprentice said, "Hodja, everyone says you're good. Does that mean that you really are good?" Hodja replied that this was not necessarily so. The boy then asked, if everyone said Hodja was bad, would it mean that he was bad? One again Hodja replied in the negative. When the apprentice enquired how he could tell, Hodja told him that if the good people said he was good and the bad people said that he was bad, then he was good. He paused for a moment, scratching his beard, and then continued, "But you know how hard it is to tell which are the good people and which are the bad."

The Turtle and the Scorpion

A scorpion approached a turtle and said, "I need your help crossing the lake. Please let me hitch a ride on your back." The turtle replied in horror, "Are you crazy? You are my mortal enemy. If I do that, you will sting me and I will die."

"Think about it," replied the scorpion. "If I sting you, we will both sink, and I, being on your back, would also drown and die. Is it logical that I would sting you?"

"I don't know," said the turtle. "Do I dare trust you?"

"Trust has nothing to do with it. It just doesn't make sense that I would sting you. Besides, I would owe you a very big favor, and you never know when that could come in handy."

"That's true," said the turtle. "All right, get on my back and I will take you across."

The scorpion leapt on the sturdy back of the turtle, and together, they swam out into the lake. When they were almost halfway across, the scorpion suddenly lashed out and stung the turtle on the neck.

"How could you do such a thing!" cried the turtle, beginning to sink. "Now we both will die!"

"Alas," said the scorpion, "I know it's strange, but I just couldn't help myself. I couldn't go against my nature."

The Soup

A neighbor came to Hodja's house from hunting, bringing a hare as a gift. Delighted, Hodja had the hare cooked into a stew and then shared it with his guest.

After that, one countryman after another started to call. Each one was a relative of the man who brought him the hare. Hodja would welcome them too, preparing the stew, even though no further presents were forthcoming. Hodja cooked some soup from the old hare stew and shared it with his guests.

At length, Hodja was exasperated. One day yet another stranger appeared.

"I am the relative of the relative who brought you the hare." He sat down, like all the rest, expecting a meal.

Hodja handed him a bowl of hot water mixed with little salt and spices.

"What kind of soup is this?" asked the stranger. "You are the relative of the relative of my neighbor, aren't you?" Hodja replied.

"Well, this is certainly the soup of the soup of the hare which was brought by him."

Two Monks Sitting by a Lake

A student went to his Zen master and said, "Master, I have been taught that all creatures have the Buddha nature—the bird that flies, the fish that swims, the butterfly, all creatures. Tell me, Master, do I have the Buddha nature?"

The master replied, "It is so. All creatures do have the Buddha nature—the bird that flies, the fish that swims, the butterfly, all creatures, except for you."

"Why, Master?" the student asks. "Why not me?"

To which the master replied, "Because you are asking this question."

The Tiger and the Strawberry

A monk was being chased by a tiger. He came to the edge of a cliff and went over the side. As he was falling, he grabbed on to a branch and held on for his life. The branch began to pull out of the cliff from its roots. Just at the moment when the branch was about to come out completely and he would plunge to his death, the monk noticed a ripe red strawberry growing right next to the branch. The monk picked the berry and ate it. It was the best-tasting strawberry he had ever had.

The Will of God

"May the Will of Allah be done," a pious man was saying about something or the other. "It always is, in any case," said Mullah Nasrudin. "How can you prove that, Mullah?" asked the man. "Quite simply, if it wasn't always being done, then surely at some time or another my will would be done, wouldn't it?"

Keep It Going

Nasrudin Hodja used to stand in the street on market days to be pointed out as an idiot. No matter how often people offered him a large and a small coin, he always chose the smaller piece. One day a kindly man said to him, "Hodja, you should take the bigger coin. Then you will have more money, and people will no longer be able to make a laughingstock of you."

"That may be true," said Hodja, "but if I always take the larger, people will stop offering me money to prove that I am more idiotic than they are. Then I would have no money at all."

The Mullah Lost His Keys

Late one night, a disciple found Mullah Nasr Eddin on his hands and knees searching for something under a lamppost.

"What are you looking for?" he asked.

"I lost my keys," replied the Mullah.

The disciple joined in the search. After what seemed like hours, he finally asked, "Mullah, are you sure you dropped your keys over here?"

Pointing into the darkness, the Mullah replied, "No, I dropped them over there." Exasperated, the disciple demanded, "Then why are we searching for them over here?"

"Well, you see," the Mullah answered, "the light is better over here."

The Beggar on the Roof

One day Hodja was repairing the tiles on the roof of his house. While he was working, a stranger knocked on his door. "What do you want?" Hodja shouted out. "Come down," replied the stranger, "so I can tell it."

Hodja put down his work, climbed down the ladder into the house, down three flights of steps, and finally opened the front door where the stranger stood. "Well," asked Hodja, "what is this important thing?"

"Could you give a little money to this poor old man?" begged the stranger.

Upset by this unfortunate man, Hodja said, "Follow me," and started up the three flights of stairs and climbed up the ladder to the roof. After the long climb, when they were both up on the roof, Hodja replied, "The answer is no!"

The Priest Who Plays Chess

In Hodja's village, there was a Greek community with a priest who enjoyed playing chess but had no one with whom to play. One day the priest decided to teach Hodja the rudiments of chess, following which, they started a game. Before they began, he crossed himself and checkmated the Hodja after a few moves.

The next time they played, the priest crossed himself and again won. After several games in which Hodja always lost, he turned to the priest and asked him whether he, too, might win if he crossed himself before each game. "Yes," replied the priest, "but first you have to learn how to play chess."

Needs

As Nasrudin Hodja emerged from the mosque after prayers, a beggar sitting on the street solicited alms. The following conversation ensued: "Are you extravagant?" asked Hodja. "Yes, Hodja" replied the beggar. "Do you like sitting around drinking coffee and smoking?" asked Hodja. "Yes," replied the beggar. "I suppose you like to go to the baths?" asked Hodja. "Yes," replied the beggar. "And maybe amuse yourself, even, by drinking with friends?" asked Hodja. "Yes, I like all those things," replied the beggar. "Tut-tut," said Hodja, and he gave him a gold piece.

A few yards farther on, another beggar who had overheard the conversation begged for alms also. "Are you extravagant?" asked Hodja. "No, Hodja," replied the second beggar. "Do you like sitting around drinking coffee and smoking?" asked Hodja. "No," replied the second beggar. "I suppose you like to go to the baths every day?" asked Hodja. "No," replied the second beggar. "And maybe amuse yourself, even, by drinking with friends?" asked Hodja. "No, I want to only live meagerly and to pray," replied the second beggar, whereupon Hodja gave him a small copper coin. "But why," wailed second beggar, "do you give me, an economical and pious man, a penny, when you give that extravagant fellow a sovereign?"

"Ah, my friend," replied Hodja, "his needs are greater than yours."

Up a Tree

A monk was high up in a tree, pruning it so it would flourish. Having finished his task, he began to scramble the long way down, carrying his tools with him. Just as he was about to step onto the last branch, before coming to the ground, his master, a much older and more experienced monk, who had been watching him the whole time, shouted, "Be careful!"

The Chess Game

A young man, who was bitterly disappointed in life, traveled to a remote monastery to ask its master a question: "I am disillusioned with life and wish to attain enlightenment. But I have no capacity for sticking to anything. I could never do the years of meditation, study, and austerity that would be required of me. I would relapse and be drawn back to the world again, painful though I know it to be. Is there any hope for me?"

"There is," said the master, "if you are really determined. Tell me what have you studied, what have you concentrated on most of your life? What have you done with yourself over the years?"

"Why, nothing really," replied the young man. "I come from a rich family, and I did not have to work. I suppose the thing I was most interested in was chess: the strategy, the winning, and losing. I spent most of my time at that."

The master thought for a moment, and then, writing a name on a slip of paper, he handed it to one of his attendants. He said, "Call this monk. Tell him to bring a chessboard and pieces." The monk soon came with the board, and the master set up the game.

He then sent for a sword and showed it to the two. He said to the monk, "You have vowed obedience to me as your master, and now I require it of you. You will play a game of chess. If you lose, I will cut off your head. I promise that you will be reborn in the pure land. If you win, I shall cut off the head of this man. Chess is the only thing he has put any effort into. If he loses, he, too, will deserve to lose his head."

They looked at the master's face and saw that he meant what he said. They began to play. From the opening moves, the youth could feel his pulse pounding in his veins, the sweat beading on his forehead. The chessboard soon became his whole world. He was entirely concentrated on it. At first, to his horror, he saw that he was losing, but then the monk made an inferior move, and he seized his chance to launch a strong attack. As his opponent's position crumbled, he looked at him. He saw a face of intelligence and sincerity, worn with years of austerity and effort. The young man thought of his own worthless life, and a wave of compassion came over him. It hardly seemed fair that such a righteous man should lose his life because of him. He deliberately made a blunder and then another, ruining his position, leaving himself defenseless.

The master suddenly leaned forward and upset the board. The two contestants sat stupefied. "There is no winner and no loser," the master said slowly. "There is no head to fall here." Turning to the young man, he said, "Only two things are required: complete concentration and compassion. Today you have learned them both. You were completely concentrated on the game, but then in that concentration, you could feel real compassion and became willing to sacrifice your life. Now stay here and pursue our training in this spirit, and your awakening is assured."

The Treasure

There was once a poor man named Isaac who had a recurring dream. He dreamt that under the eastern bridge leading into the capitol, someone had buried a great treasure and that he should go there and dig it up.

Finally, after having the same dream, night after night, for more than a week, he decided to make the journey to the capitol city and find the treasure.

Upon arriving in the city, he went directly to the eastern bridge. It was exactly as it had appeared in his dream, but the bridge was guarded day and night, so he dared not dig under it. Nevertheless, he went to the bridge every morning, walking back and forth and around it until evening, hoping for a chance to go under the bridge unseen and dig for the treasure.

The captain of the guards, who had begun to take notice of Isaac as he wandered around the bridge, approached him and asked in a kindly way whether he was waiting for someone or looking for something.

Isaac, embarrassed by his own foolishness, sheepishly confessed to the captain that he had come from very far away and told him about his dream.

The captain, laughing, said, "So, because of this dream you had, you poor fellow, you travelled for weeks just to come here? If I were as foolish as you, I would listen to a dream of my own and go to a little town around two weeks journey from here and seek out a poor man named Isaac, look under his hearth, and there I should find all the wealth I would need for the rest of my life."

Isaac bowed to the captain and set off on his long journey home. When he arrived home, two weeks later, he went to the hearth in his kitchen, moved the hearthstone, and found the treasure he had seen in his dream.

The Perfect Wife

Mullah Nasrudin was sitting in a tea shop when a friend came excitedly to speak with him. "I'm about to get married, Mullah," his friend stated, "and I'm very excited. Mullah, have you ever thought of marriage yourself?" Nasrudin replied, "I did think of getting married. In my youth, in fact, I very much wanted to do so. I waited to find for myself the perfect wife. I traveled looking for her, first to Damascus. There I met a beautiful woman who was gracious, kind, and deeply spiritual, but she had no worldly knowledge. I traveled further and went to Isphahan. There I met a woman who was both spiritual and worldly, beautiful in many ways, but we did not communicate well. Finally, I went to Cairo, and there after much searching, I found her. She was spiritually deep, graceful, and beautiful in every respect, at home in the world and at home in the realms beyond it. I felt I had found the perfect wife."

His friend questioned further, "Then why did you not marry her, Mullah?"

"Alas," said Nasrudin as he shook his head, "she was, unfortunately, waiting for the perfect husband."

The Magician's Sheep

There is an Eastern tale, which speaks about a very rich magician who had a great many sheep. But at the same time, the magician was also very mean. He did not want to hire shepherds, nor did he want to erect a fence about the pasture where his sheep were grazing. The sheep consequently often wandered into the forest, fell into ravines, and so on, and above all, they ran away, for they knew that the magician wanted their flesh and skins, and this they did not like.

At last, the magician found a remedy. He hypnotized his sheep and suggested to them that they were immortal and that no harm was being done to them when they were skinned, that, on the contrary, it would be very good for them and even pleasant. Secondly, he suggested that the magician was a good master who loved his flock so much that he was ready to do anything in the world for them. In the third place, he suggested to them that if anything at all was going to happen to them, it was not going to happen just then, at any rate not that day, and therefore, they had no need to think about it. Further, the magician suggested to his sheep that they were not sheep at all; to some of them, he suggested that they were lions, to others that they were eagles, to others that they were men, and to others that they were magicians.

Those Who Know

The Mullah was invited to speak in front of a great congregation. It was not something he wished to do. After much discussion, he was finally convinced to appear. When it was announced that he was going to speak, everyone in the town came to hear his wisdom.

There was a hush over the crowd as the Mullah walked to the platform. The Mullah looked out over his captive audience and asked, "Do you know what I am going to speak about tonight?" No one did.

"Then I am wasting my time," said the Mullah and walked out of the building.

The congregants were stunned. They demanded that the Mullah must be made to return the next week and fulfill his obligation. The Mullah once again had to be persuaded but, after much cajoling, finally agreed.

Once again, he asked, "Do you know what I am going to speak about tonight?"

This time, the members of the congregation were prepared, and they all answered yes; they knew what he was going to speak about.

"Then I am wasting your time," said the Mullah and, again, walked out of the building.

The congregants were outraged and demanded that the Mullah be made to appear once again. The Mullah condescended to appear one last time.

That night, the members of the congregation agreed that if the same question was asked, half of them would say yes and the other half would say no.

The Mullah appeared and once again asked, "Do you know what I am going to speak about tonight?"

As they had planned, half the audience said no and the other half said yes.

"Good," said the Mullah, "those who know, tell those who don't know," and walked out.

The Leaky Pot

There was an old woman who, every morning, would walk down to the well of the village and, as was the custom, fill her two waterpots, which she carried on a pole across her shoulders.

One of the pots had a crack in it, and by the time the woman would reach her home, the cracked pot would be practically empty. This made the pot very sad, because it felt that it was not worth anything.

Finally, when the pot could not bear its shame any longer, it asked the woman why she kept carrying it, even though it could no longer carry the water back to the woman's home.

With great gentleness, the woman explained, "You do not understand. If you look on your side of the path, you will see beautiful flowers, which are enjoyed by everyone in the village. These flowers would surely die if you did not leak, for it is you who are watering them and keeping them healthy."

Members Only

Innocently unaware of the prejudices held against him, an old black man, staunchly religious, applied for membership in an exclusive church. The pastor attempted to put him off with all sorts of evasive remarks. The old man, aware that he was not wanted, said that he would pray on it and perhaps the Lord would tell him just what to do.

Several days later, he returned. "Well," asked the minister, "did the Lord send you a message?"

"Yes, sir. He did," was the answer. "He told me that it wasn't any use trying. He also told me that for more than ten years, He's been trying to get into that same church, and they still won't let Him in."

Things Could Always Be Worse

There was once a very poor farmer who lived in a tiny hut with his wife, three small children, and his mother-in-law. His mother-in-law was always complaining vociferously about one thing or another. The children would be shouting, screaming, and constantly fighting with each other without end. Also his wife was always nagging and carping at him or yelling at the children. The poor man could find no peace.

Finally, when he felt he could not stand it for one more day, he went to his rabbi for advice. The rabbi stroked his beard and thought deeply for a while. After some time, he asked the farmer if he had any chickens. The farmer replied that yes, indeed, he did have six chickens and a very fine rooster also. "Good," said the rabbi, "I want you to take the chickens and rooster into your hut to live with you." The farmer began to protest, but the rabbi insisted and asked for his trust. So the chickens and rooster were brought into the hut.

Things in the hut were far from being better; they were much worse! After only two days, the farmer went back to his rabbi complaining about how bad the situation had become. The rabbi then asked the farmer if he had a goat. The farmer replied that he did. "Good," said the rabbi, "take the goat inside your hut with you and let him live there also." The farmer could not understand how this could make things better but, respecting the rabbi's wisdom, did as he was told.

As you could well imagine, living conditions inside the hut were near intolerable! With the chickens squawking, the goat eating everything in sight, the children screaming, the wife nagging, and the mother-in-law's constant complaining, the farmer was fit to be tied!

The very next day, the farmer went back to the rabbi to complain about this intolerable situation. The rabbi asked him, "Do you perhaps maybe also own a cow?" To this, the farmer dejectedly answered that, yes, he did. "Good," said the rabbi, "take the cow inside and let him live there also." The farmer was beside himself but once again trusted the rabbi and did as he was told.

What chaos! The chickens were squawking, the goat was eating everything in sight, the children were screaming, his wife was nagging, his mother-in-law was constantly complaining, and now the cow was lowing—to say nothing about the feathers flying, the extreme overcrowding, and the smell! The farmer was about to lose his mind!

Rushing back to the rabbi, the farmer begged for another solution to this hell on earth. Seeing that this was all that the farmer could bear, the rabbi instructed him to remove all the animals from the hut. The next day, the farmer returned to the rabbi and, with great humility, said, "Thank you, Rabbi, for your wise counsel. Never in my entire life have I known such peace and quiet as I now have in my home."

The Angel of Death

A Sufi was at home one day when his friend Abdullah burst into his room. "You must lend me fifty kopeks immediately," he said. "I was having coffee in the café in the marketplace when I suddenly saw the angel of death sitting at a table. He kept staring at me! I feel he has come to take me. I must leave here immediately and go to Medina. That's far enough away. I'll be safe there. You must loan me the money for the fare." The Sufi gave him the money and, after Abdullah departed, began to think. "I've never seen the angel of death. It might be possible to meet him and even learn something from him." He put on his coat and went down to the café in market-place hoping the angel of death was still there. He searched the café until he saw him sitting at a table in the darkest corner of the cafe. The Sufi went over, introduced himself, and asked, "Are you really the angel of death?" The man nodded. The Sufi then inquired if it would be possible to speak with him for a while. "I'm sorry," said the angel of death, "but I have to leave right now. You see, this afternoon I have an appointment in Medina, with a man named Abdullah."

The Coconut

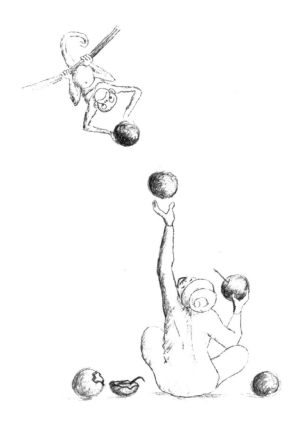

When a monkey throws a coconut at a wise man, instead of reacting and throwing it back at the monkey, the wise man drinks the milk, eats the meat, and even makes a bowl out of the shell.

Two Wives

One evening, an old Cherokee warrior was talking to his grandson. He told him of a battle that is waged inside every human.

He said, "My son, the battle is between two wolves inside of us all. One is evil—filled with anger, envy, jealousy, sorrow, lies, regret, greed, arrogance, self-pity, guilt, resentment, inferiority, lies, false pride, violence, superiority, and ego."

"The other is good—filled with joy, peace, love, hope, serenity, humility, kindness, benevolence, empathy, generosity, truth, compassion, and faith."

His grandson thought about this for a while and finally asked, "Grandfather, which one wins the battle?"

The old warrior smiled and replied, "The one that you feed."

Chasing the Devil

A rabbi leaving his meditation room noticed his eldest disciples engaged in a very heated and animated discussion. Later, he asked one of them, "What were you all conversing about so passionately?" The disciple answered, "We were arguing about whether we have yet reached a level at which the devil has stopped chasing us."

"No, no, no," he chuckled. "Certainly none of you are that advanced yet. You are all still chasing him!"

The Cricket

While walking along a busy city street with one of his disciples, an old monk stopped suddenly in his tracks. "I hear a cricket," he said to his companion. "That's impossible." The young monk replied. "There are no crickets in the city. Besides, with all the noise of the people and traffic, even if there was a cricket around, you would not be able to hear it chirp."

"All the same, I hear a cricket," the old monk insisted and proceeded to cross the street toward a tree that occupied a small portion of the sidewalk. Next to the tree was a small amount of grass sharing the tree's space. The monk bent down and parted the blades of grass. Sure enough, hiding in the grass was a cricket chirping its song. The younger monk was stunned. "You must have remarkable hearing!" he said to his master. "No better than anyone else has," he replied. "I will prove to you that all these people rushing past us have the same ability." He then reached into his pocket and took out a few coins, which he then tossed on to the sidewalk. As the coins hit the ground, making the sound we are all familiar with, all the people passing by stopped and turned to find the loose change. "You see," said the old monk, "it is just a matter of what you are listening for."

The Pilgrimage

It is a Muslim's obligation that once in their life to make the hajj, a pilgrimage to Mecca. One family was setting out on just such a journey; there was great activity in the home. The grandmother, well into her nineties, was also gathering clothes and bedding. At that point, her grandson came in and, seeing her preparing for the journey, asked, "Granny, what are you doing?"

"I'm preparing for the hajj," she replied. Sympathetically, the grandson explained, "Granny, it is wonderful you want to come, but we'll be riding in the caravan all day long, every day for weeks. We'll be sleeping in tents or on the ground. There won't be rest or bathrooms." Meanwhile, the grandmother's son, overhearing, came in. As his mother, smiling to herself, continued to make ready for the journey, the son continued, "Mother, you can't come on this journey. It is too dangerous. I'm sure we'll have more than our share of adventures, and even the weather is ominous. It is arduous for someone young and fit to make the pilgrimage, so I'm sorry, but you just can't come along." The grandmother looked at her son and grandson and said, "It seems you don't understand the point of the hajj." A look of bemusement crossed over the son's face. "Why don't you tell us the point of the hajj." The grandmother replied, "The point of the hajj is not to reach Mecca but to prepare one's self at each step of the way."

Gates of Heaven

A man died and found himself in front of the gates of heaven. The looming golden gates were all that stood in front of him and what he had struggled his whole life to achieve. He found a small old man with a long flowing white beard sitting on a high stool next to the great gates. The man stood bewildered in front of him. "Is this heaven?" asked the man.

"Not yet, the gates will open sometime today. I don't remember exactly when. I'm old, and I forget such things, but you qualify. I see it here in the ledger. A lot of good deeds. I'm very impressed, and you followed all the commandments. Very good," the old man replied.

"The door opens, and I just go in?" the man asked.

"Not exactly," the old man spoke with a twinkle in his eyes. "The doors only open for a moment, and you only get one chance to enter, that's it! We get a lot of people who qualify. Best of luck."

"Thanks," the man said, as the old man hobbled over to his high stool and quickly fell into a deep restful sleep. The man sat down in front of the great golden gates and waited. "I will watch these doors every moment of the day. I will not lose what I have struggled for my whole life."

The day passed, and in the middle of the afternoon, a great butterfly came and sat on the man's hand. He had never seen such a beautiful butterfly, and he looked down on it affectionately, but when he looked up, the gates of heaven were just closing.

Did We Get It Right?

One day, it was discovered that on a remote island in the Caspian Sea, there existed a monastery that had been out of touch with the main body of the Eastern Orthodox Church for as far back as anyone could remember. After a while, the church decided to send an emissary to the island to make sure that the monks there were still adhering to the correct forms of prayer and worship. The emissary, a priest, found the monks sincere and especially devout, but many of the prayers were in the wrong order. At times, when they were meant to kneel, they stood. Where they were to say "Amen," they said, "Lord, have mercy," and so on. After showing them all the errors they were making and instructing them in the correct practices, he felt very satisfied that he had put them back on the right path. The next day, he left on the boat he had arrived on, and as it made its way out to sea, he stood by the rail and congratulated himself on showing them the way. Suddenly, he heard a shout. Looking up, he couldn't believe his eyes. In the distance he could see one of the monks running on top of the water toward the boat! When the monk caught up to the priest's boat, he looked at the priest and asked, "Sir, we were confused about one of the things you told us. Did you say to do the morning prayers at 6:00 a.m. or at 7:00?"

The Greatest Gift

Would you like to save the world from the degradation
and destruction it seems destined for?
Then step away from shallow mass movements and
quietly go to work on your own self-awareness.

If you want to awaken all of humanity, then awaken all of
yourself. If you want to eliminate the suffering in the world,
then eliminate all that is dark and negative in yourself.

Truly, the greatest gift you have to give is
that of your own transformation.

—Lao Tzu

Two Things

There are only two things in the universe.
Matter and there's...

it doesn't matter.

Illustrations

Acknowledgements

All the members of the Brewster groups throughout the past forty years, they are the ones who searched for these stories and shared them at our celebrations.

Thank you, Gary Strum, for all his time and effort in organizational skills.

Bruce Zeines for his efforts in the production of so many illustrations, his thoughts about what the design should be, and his friendship.

John Anderson for his continual encouragement.

Rob Cohen, without his computer skills, this book would never have come to fruition.

CPSIA information can be obtained
at www.ICGtesting.com
Printed in the USA
LVHW072323190421
684984LV00016B/217